STEP-UP
ART AND DESIGN

Talking Textiles

Susan Ogier

Cherrytree Books are distributed in the
United States by Black Rabbit Books
P.O. Box 3263
Mankato, MN 56002

U.S. publication copyright © Cherrytree Books 2009

Printed in China by WKT Co. Ltd.

Library of Congress Cataloging-in-Publication Data
Ogier, Susan.
  Talking textiles / Susan Ogier. -- 1st ed.
    p. cm. -- (Step-up art and design)
  Includes index.
  ISBN 978-1-84234-574-0 (hardcover)
  1. Textile crafts--Juvenile literature. I. Title. II. Series.

TT699.O32 2010
746--dc22

                                    2008044123

13-digit ISBN: 9781842345740

First Edition
9 8 7 6 5 4 3 2 1

First published in 2008 by Evans Brothers Ltd.
2A Portman Mansions, Chiltern Street,
London W1U 6NR, United Kingdom

Produced for Evans Brothers Limited by
White-Thomson Publishing Ltd

Acknowledgments:

Special thanks to Mrs. Pat Allen and the teachers and pupils in
Years 3, 4, 5 and 6 at St. Luke's Primary School, Kingston upon
Thames, Surrey, UK, for all their artwork and help in the
preparation of this book.

Picture acknowledgments:

Alamy: page 6t (M. L. Pearson). Bridgeman Art Library: pages
8t (Victoria & Albert Museum, London, UK), 8b (Musee de la
Tapisserie, Bayeux, France, with special authorization of the
city of Bayeux), 11l (Private Collection, © Philip Mould Ltd).
Corbis: pages 12b (Blaine Harrington III), 17b (Stapleton
Collection), 20b (Penny Tweedie), 22b (John and Lisa Merrill),
24 (Christie's Images), 25t (Adrian Bradshaw/epa). Ecoscene:
page 27 (Ed Maynard). Chris Fairclough: cover (main), pages
7t&b, 9, 11r, 13l&r, 15b, 17t, 18, 19l&r, 21t&b, 23, 28r, 29r.
Istockphoto: cover tr, title page, pages 4t, 4bl&r, 5 (all), 10tl&r,
10bl, 15t, 20t, 28l, 29l. Kobal Collection: page 12t
(Columbia). Shutterstock: pages 4c, 6b, 10br, 14 (all), 16t&b,
22t, 25b, 26t. Neil Thomson: cover tl, page 26b.

Contents

What are Textiles?

People have been making textiles for thousands of years. Textiles are used to make clothes and furnishings for our homes, such as curtains, carpets, sheets, and blankets, and in art and craftwork. Other uses include bags, tents, sails for boats, and handkerchiefs—can you think of any more?

Making Textiles

Textiles are made from fibers. These fibers are first spun into yarn and then bound together to make a textile. Different methods are used to bind the yarn—these include knitting, crochet, lacemaking, braiding, felting, and weaving (see page 6).

▲ A knitted textile is made by using two knitting needles to make and connect loops in the yarn.

▼ In crochet, loops in the yarn are made and connected with one hooked needle.

▶ Lace is a delicate textile made by looping and twisting yarn into patterns.

▶ Braiding is plaiting three or more strands of yarn to make a strip. Here, strips of braiding have been joined to make a rug.

Textile Sources

Textiles are made from either natural or synthetic fibers. Natural fibers may come from plants, such as the cotton plant and flax (which makes linen), or from animals, for example wool. Synthetic fibers are made from chemicals and are used to create textiles such as nylon and Lycra.

Materials Collage

Collect as many different types of textiles as you can. Try to choose examples that show the different ways that fibers can be connected to make the textile, such as knitted, laced, or felted. Make a collage in your sketchbook and write notes next to the materials saying which method you think has been used.

▲ *This cyclist is wearing Lycra. Why do you think this material is suitable for sports activities?*

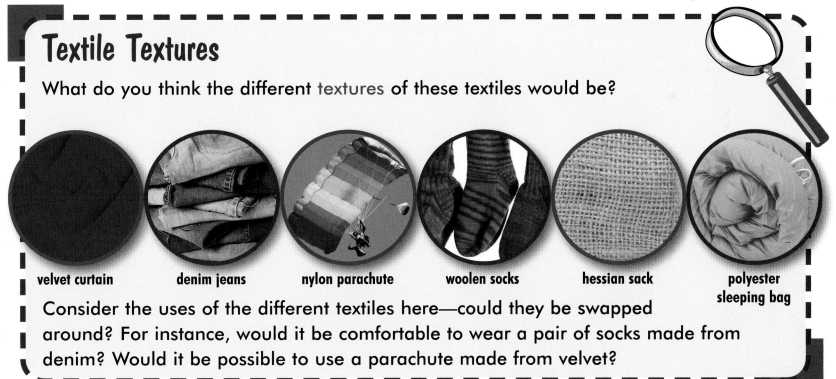

Textile Textures

What do you think the different textures of these textiles would be?

| velvet curtain | denim jeans | nylon parachute | woolen socks | hessian sack | polyester sleeping bag |

Consider the uses of the different textiles here—could they be swapped around? For instance, would it be comfortable to wear a pair of socks made from denim? Would it be possible to use a parachute made from velvet?

Spinning and Weaving

Spinning is the process of making fibers into lengths of stronger yarn. This yarn can then be used to create a textile, for example by weaving.

Spinning

Do you remember the story of Sleeping Beauty, who pricked her finger on a spinning wheel and slept for a hundred years? Before the invention of the spinning wheel, people twisted the fibers together by hand to make yarn. Modern spinning machines are powered by electricity and can produce yards of yarn every second.

Weaving

Weaving has been used to create textiles since ancient times. A weaver uses a machine called a loom to make a textile by interlocking lengths of yarn called warp, which run horizontally, and weft, which run vertically.

▶ Can you see how the warp and weft are interlocked to create this woven fiber canvas?

▲ *This girl is using a spinning wheel to make woolen yarn from the fleece of a sheep.*

Once Upon a Time...

The crafts of spinning and weaving are central to many myths and fairy tales, for example *Rumpelstiltskin* and *Sleeping Beauty*. Write a fairy story for younger children around the theme of spinning or weaving. How will you illustrate your story?

Making a Large-scale Weaving

Make a weaving, based on a myth or fairy story, with a small group of friends.

First, agree on the story to use. Read it out loud, trying to visualize colors, sounds, and images as you are reading. Note these ideas in your sketchbooks.

You will need to work collaboratively to decide how the different ideas will work together in one piece of work. Agree on a final design.

Staple some garden netting to an empty wooden frame. Then collect materials that are suitable for threading in and out of the netting and that reflect the ideas in the final design. These could include ribbon or strips of fabric, crêpe paper, tissue, wrapping paper, and recycled materials such as plastics. You could even tie related objects into your weaving to add interest.

We're creating a river by weaving in lots of different blues and silvers.

I think that the frame we added makes the weaving look really special.

Tales from Tapestries

Many different cultures have used weaving to create textiles. The Incas wrapped dead bodies in elaborate woven textiles before burial. The Egyptians, Greeks and Romans decorated their homes with wall hangings of intricate woven designs. In a tapestry, the threads of yarn are woven together in a special way to make a pattern or picture. Tapestries are often used to tell stories.

The Bayeux Tapestry

The Bayeux Tapestry is 230 feet long and tells the story of King Harold and the Battle of Hastings. This 900-year-old piece of work is not actually a tapestry at all because it is embroidered. A true tapestry is woven.

▲ This 15th-century tapestry is one of a series known as the Devonshire Hunting Tapestries and would have been used to decorate and insulate the cold stone homes of rich people. Look carefully at the story in the tapestry. Why do you think medieval people liked this type of subject matter?

▶ This scene from the Bayeux Tapestry shows Harold's death, but it is not clear how he dies. Many historians now think that Harold is not the figure with an arrow in the eye, but the one cut down by a horseman.

News Collage

Cartoons tell a story in sequence—just like the Bayeux Tapestry. Choose a current news story and create a cartoon by showing it in three or four stages. Your cartoon will be the starting point for a collage made from textiles.

Refer to your cartoon to order the news story as a clear sequence of events. Split into pairs or small groups and decide who will make a collage of which scene.

For each scene, collect a variety of materials that you can flatten and shape by cutting and tearing. Arrange your shapes on a piece of cardboard or fabric. When you are happy with your composition, secure the pieces with glue or thread. Add texture and detail by using string and wool, which can be glued to your collage or sewn through the base and knotted or taped at the back.

This cartoon represents a news story from China, when the worst snowstorm in years left hundreds of thousands of people stranded at train stations.

When all the collage scenes are complete, display your news story by placing them in sequence alongside your cartoon.

Clothes and Fashion

Humans have always needed to protect their bodies from the weather and from harm. Early people used animal skins and plant material to make clothes for themselves. There is evidence that Stone Age people sewed items together using needles made from bone or wood.

Changing Fashions

The clothes we wear today are not simply to protect us from injury or the weather, but they also give messages to other people about who we are or what we do. "Fashion" means the style in clothing that is popular or admired at a particular time. Fashions are always changing, as we can see when we look back at some of the clothes that people wore in the past.

Today we have a lot of choice and can easily find clothes that we feel comfortable in, whatever our personal tastes. What fashions or styles do you like?

1950s 1960s 1980s 1920s

▶ *These fashions all date from the 20th century. Can you match each picture to a decade?*

Galleries and Museums

One way to find out about fashions of the past is to visit museums that have collections of historic costumes and galleries to look at portrait paintings. Portraits that show clothes, jewelry, and hairstyles tell us what fashions were like in different periods. Modern fashion designers are also often inspired by fashions of the past.

Fashion for a Friend

Design an outfit for a friend that shows his or her personality. Find out more about your friend by interviewing him or her and asking about likes and dislikes. What colors will you use? You might choose yellows and oranges for someone who has a bubbly personality or purples and grays for someone who is thoughtful. What materials and textures will you use? Note down all your ideas in your sketchbook.

Use fabric or newspaper to make the outfit by sewing, gluing and taping pieces together. How will the outfit fasten together? You might consider making a cape that goes around the shoulders or a tabard that slips over the head.

Perhaps you could organize a fashion show for the rest of the school and photograph everyone in their new designs.

◄ *Do you think that Queen Elizabeth I looks comfortable in this 17th-century fashion? The richness of her dress and jewelry showed everyone her great power, wealth, and status in society.*

Roughed up hair

Hairspray scrunch

Big belt

Blue and pink goes well

Flares

Cotton hoody with orange stripes

Flexy shiny plastic

Shell

Denim jeans dotty

▲ *Use your sketchbook to draw your initial ideas after interviewing your friend. You could design an outfit for an everyday or a special occasion.*

What a Performance!

Costumes are an important part of any performance, whether it is a dance or a drama, and good costume design helps the audience to become more involved in the story.

Setting the Scene

Have you been to a play or a pantomime or seen one on the television? How did the costumes help to create the mood? If you have been a performer in a dance or play, how did your costume help you to understand or develop your role?

Carnival Arts

Performances do not always take place inside a theater, and sometimes they require the audience to participate as well as watch. Carnival is an example of an art form that takes place outdoors, and is as much about the imaginative costumes as it is about the music, dance, and participation. The name is from the Italian "Carnevale," which means "to put away the meat." This comes from a time when people held costumed parties before they gave up eating meat for Lent.

▲ Period costumes can help an audience to place a film or play in its historical setting.

◄ Carnivals take place in many cities of the world. These stilt-walkers are taking part in a Children's Carnival in Trinidad, an island in the Caribbean.

Carnival Creation

Work with a partner to design a three-dimensional headpiece for a carnival performer. Start by measuring your head size and then make a simple cardboard band, stapling it to fit correctly. You will create your headpiece by building attachments on to this base.

Design your headpiece on paper first, being as imaginative as possible. Then create the shape of your design by bending materials such as wire, cardboard, and paper, and fixing them to the card band. Add decoration with paint, foil, feathers, ribbons, beads, and flowers.

Artist's practice

The designers of elaborate carnival costumes must consider that the person wearing the costume will be moving and dancing all the time. Testing and evaluating the design at all stages is very important.

My headpiece was based on ideas that I had while we were studying the Ancient Egyptians.

Evaluate your work often and change things as you are working. Talk to your friends and look at their work, too, as this will help you develop your own ideas.

13

Investigating Pattern

Pattern is all around us and is an important part of how we live our lives. The rising and setting of the sun, the seasons of the year, and our daily routines all follow patterns. Visually, pattern occurs in both the natural and the built world, and this has interested artists from many cultures throughout history.

Art and Math

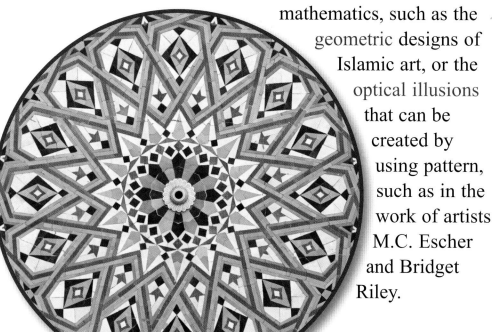

Some artworks use pattern in a way that is more related to mathematics, such as the geometric designs of Islamic art, or the optical illusions that can be created by using pattern, such as in the work of artists M.C. Escher and Bridget Riley.

▲ Look at the repetition in this Islamic design. Which basic geometric shapes are used to create this complicated pattern?

▼ Nature creates amazing patterns. Artists are able to use these natural patterns to inspire their own work.

Observation

Look for patterns around you. Try to spot the less obvious examples, such as the patterns created by table or chair legs, an arrangement of window panes or a stack of books. Sketch the more surprising discoveries in your sketchbook.

Virtual Patterns

Try these pattern activities. Paint a symmetrical pattern on a virtual wall at: http://www.nga.gov/kids/zone/wallovers. htm and design your own tartan at: http://www.vam.ac.uk/vastatic/microsites/ 1231_vivienne_westwood/tartan.html

Cut and Stick

Collect samples of printed patterns from magazines, wallpaper, fabric samples, or wrapping paper and make a collage of them in your sketchbook. Make written notes to remind yourself where you found the pattern or ways in which it might be used. What are the differences between the printed patterns and the ones that you discovered from looking around you?

Patterns for Interior Design

Designing, furnishing, and decorating the insides of our homes is called interior design. Patterns are often used in interior design. Look around your own home and list the places where you find examples of patterns. This might include woven patterns—for example, on blankets and carpets—or printed patterns—for example, on curtains or wallpaper. Perhaps floor or wall tiles have been arranged to form a pattern.

Floor Coverings

Today we have the choice of whether we want carpets or another floor covering in our homes, but in the 17th century, only the very rich could afford the luxury of a carpet. At this time, intricately designed carpets were being handmade by craftsmen in Persia by a painstaking method where tufts were threaded and tied individually.

▲ *Look carefully to find as many patterns as you can in this picture of a bedroom. Don't forget to include the patterns that you see in the objects and furniture.*

◀ *Modern Persian carpets are made by machine rather than by hand. They are usually made of wool and are highly patterned and very colorful.*

Design your Own Wallpaper

Decorative wallpapers are made up of a pattern that is repeated all over the paper. The pattern may be very small, and repeated often, or it may be very large.

Try making your own wallpaper. First design the pattern that will be repeated to make a length of wallpaper. In your sketchbook, try out different color combinations and ensure there is contrast in tone between your background color and your image in the foreground.

Now make a sturdy cardboard template of the pattern. Glue string and cardboard shapes to the base to create the pattern. Paint your background color on to a wall-length piece of lining paper using a decorating roller. When this has dried, use your contrasting color or colors to paint over your template, and print your pattern on to the wallpaper several times. This is called block printing.

▶ *When your wallpaper is dry, you might like to add some hand-drawn details with pastels. Naomi used white pastel to draw the stems on to her flower/leaf printed pattern.*

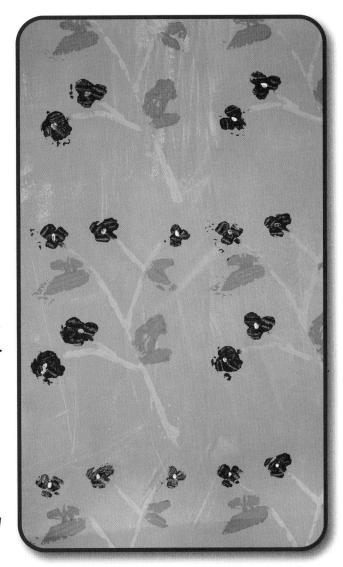

William Morris

William Morris was a British artist known for his wallpaper and tapestry designs. He was also an architect, poet and writer. Find out more about William Morris and then test your knowledge with the quiz at:
http://www1.walthamforest.gov.uk/wmg/child.htm

The World of Work

Art and design are important aspects of the world of work and it can be very interesting to have a visit from a real artist or designer whose job it is to create new things for us to use.

Meet a Designer

Textile designers have to invent new and exciting fabrics that will make us want to buy them. Zoe, a textile designer, has come to show a Year 6 class her textile designs that have been sold in shops.

▶ *The children are interested in how Zoe develops her ideas, so she is showing them her sketchbook, as well as some of her finished designs.*

Small Details

Look at home for designs in some unusual places. Perhaps there might be a design in the lining of a coat or on the back of a chair. Small details like this can make an object more attractive and desirable.

Inspiration

Zoe shows the children how she looks for inspiration in existing products and designs by looking at art, objects, and materials from the past. When she sees something she likes, she makes sketches and notes in her sketchbook, and this is how her ideas begin to develop.

Design Brief

The children are going to work in the same way as Zoe, and create a design by choosing an object they like to use as a starting point.

First, they make careful drawings of the object in their sketchbooks. Next, they simplify the drawings by using outlines to concentrate on the shapes and patterns. They use these shapes and patterns to create the final design.

I adapted the design we made with Zoe to make a potato print for my t-shirt.

▲ *Zoe helps the children try out their designs by making monoprints. They roller black ink on to a smooth surface and place paper over the top very lightly. They draw the simplified design on to the paper and carefully lift it off the inked surface. The design idea is now ready to be used on other materials.*

Batik and Tie Dye

Color has been used in textiles for thousands of years. Batik and tie dye are forms of resist dyeing, which means that some areas of the textile are treated to resist, or repel, dye. These areas show up as a design once the textile has been dipped into a dye bath or painted with fabric paints.

Equipment

With tie dye, tightly tied string acts as a mask, preventing the dye from staining the textile underneath. Batik uses hot wax in the same way and this is painted on to the textile with either a brush or a special drawing tool, called a tjanting. When batik items are mass produced, a metal stamping tool is used to cover large areas of fabric very quickly.

A Colorful World

Traditionally, dye colors were obtained from natural sources—plants or animals. The leaf of the indigo plant can be dried and crushed to make blue/purple, the spice turmeric and flowers such as marigolds make good yellows, and the cochineal beetle, when it has been dried and crushed, produces a vibrant red. We now also have synthetic dyes created by chemicals in factories to provide us with a huge range of colors.

◀ *Colorful tie dye makes great fashion items. The white lines on this T-shirt show where the fabric was masked by tightly tied string.*

▼ *The patterns on batik are very different from those on tie dyed fabric. What differences can you see between the two examples shown here?*

Flour Paste Batik

Make your own resist paste by mixing enough water to flour to make a smooth, creamy consistency. Add a few drops of glycerine to help soften the mixture.

Tape some fabric to an empty frame, or piece of board, and paint the paste on in a design of your choice. You could also create flowing lines by squeezing the mixture from plastic bottles. Allow the paste to dry thoroughly overnight.

The next day, use fabric paint or dyes to add color. When this is dry, remove the fabric from the frame and scrape or rub away the paste before washing, drying and ironing the batik. You could put it back on the frame to display it.

▼ Tamay is using fabric dyes to achieve a strong, lasting color on her batik.

▶ *Tamay looked at pictures of the African landcape to inspire her batik design. This type of batik is traditionally an African technique where leaves from cassava plants are crushed to form a paste.*

Safety

Always wear protective clothing when using dyes, and take care when using a hot iron.

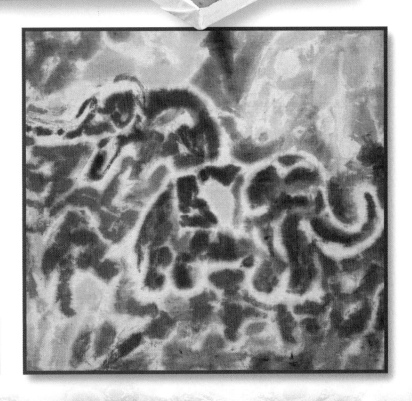

Quilting and Appliqué

Quilting is created by sewing layers of fabric together. Appliqué is the stitching of pieces of fabric or other materials on to a textile to create decorative designs.

Folk Art

Today, crafts such as appliqué and quilting are seen as folk art. It is usually women who practice them, often within a local social group. Some areas in the world, such as Latin and South America, are well known for their work in quilting and appliqué.

▲ *This picture shows fabric being sewn on to a quilt, using the appliqué method. Can you find examples of appliqué at home? Look on items such as cushion covers or clothing.*

Art and Politics

Arpilleras, which are textile pictures showing daily life, originated in Chile, South America, in the 1970s. Women who had been made prisoners by the government of the time made them. The women used the arpilleras to tell their stories to the outside world. They also used them to send secret messages to their friends, by sewing the messages into pockets underneath the appliquéd designs.

Arpilleras are still made in South America today and sales are an important part of the economy in many small neighborhoods. ▲

Discussion Point

The prison guards did not check the arpilleras because they did not think the arpilleras could be important. Why do you think the guards were not suspicious of the women's work? Do you think the women used this to their own advantage?

Your Own Story

Draw scenes from everyday life in your area in your sketchbook. Perhaps you live near a street market or have a local street where you can watch people going about their daily business.

Gather a wide variety of materials, such as felt, fabric squares, braiding, net, and silks, for gluing and sewing to create an appliqué that tells the story of your local area. You will need to think about the sizes and shapes of pieces of fabric, and try different arrangements before you stick and sew them into place.

Review the work regularly. Is your work telling the story that you wanted it to?

▼ *In your sketches, pay attention to the elements of color, texture, pattern, and shape.*

The Story of Silk

Silk is a luxurious textile that was first developed in China at least 5,000 years ago. It is made from silk fiber, which comes from the cocoon of the silkworm.

▶ *This glamorous robe from China is made from fur-lined silk and is decorated with beautiful embroidery. Who do you think might have owned an article of clothing such as this?*

Mystery Story

There is still a lot of mystery surrounding the origins of silk. According to legend, it was discovered by Hsi Ling Shi, the 14-year-old wife of the emperor, Huang Ti. In one version of the legend, she was drinking tea under a mulberry tree and a silkworm cocoon fell into her tea cup. As she lifted it out, the fiber of the cocoon started to unravel. She then had the idea to weave the fiber and she had discovered silk.

Strong and Long

The silk fiber that comes from the unraveled cocoon of the silk worm is as strong as steel of the same thickness, and one cocoon can yield more than 1,000 yards of silk yarn.

Secret

The method of silk production was a tightly kept secret in China for around 3,000 years, and for anyone disclosing that secret, or smuggling silkworm eggs out of the country, the penalty was a death sentence.

Silk became a highly valuable product for trading, even as valuable as gold.

Silkworms

Silkworms are the pupae or caterpillars of silk moths. If the pupa is allowed to metamorphose into an adult moth, the silk threads are destroyed. In commercial silk production, only moths that will be needed to breed are allowed to live. Over the years, the silk moth has lost its ability to either eat or fly even though it has a wingspan of about 2 inches (50mm).

▶ *Silkworms are still cultivated on farms today and they are very labor-intensive for the farm workers. They need to eat huge quantities of mulberry leaves and are very sensitive to noise, smells, and temperature.*

Experiment

Painting on a fabric such as silk feels very different to painting on paper, as silk is much more absorbent. Experiment by painting a design on some different fabrics. You could use silk, denim, cotton, canvas, velvet, and patterned fabric, such as curtain samples. What else can you think of?

Try different qualities of paint, such as watercolor, acrylic, or powder, to see which is the most successful on the different surfaces. Which effects do you like the best? Stick the experiments in your sketchbook and make notes beside them describing the results.

◀ *Look at the simple design on this silk painting. It looks as if the artist worked quickly, but he or she planned the composition and colors carefully before starting to paint.*

Recycling Textiles

We are all becoming very aware of our responsibility to look after the world and its resources. One of the simplest things that we can do to help is to recycle our used goods and to encourage our families to do the same.

▶ *People throw away millions of tons of textiles every year, most of which goes into landfill sites. A great deal of this could be easily reused or recycled.*

Reuse and Recycle

More than 70 per cent of the world's population wears secondhand clothes. Good-quality unwanted clothes can be sold in thrift stores or yard sales. Specialist companies can recycle old items of clothing that are too old or threadbare to be wearable. Recycled textiles can be made into cloths for wiping and cleaning, or used for padding and stuffing in furniture.

▶ *This colorful rag doll was made for sale in India from offcut scraps from a T-shirt factory. The arms and legs were made from circles of fabric threaded on to stretchy elastic. The facial features were also cut from tiny scraps and glued in place.*

You can take your unwanted clothes, bedlinen and curtains to a textile bank. These will then go to a sorting center like the one in this picture. They will be graded for quality and then sent to thrift stores, sold overseas, or recycled.

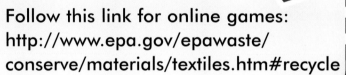

More on Recycling

Follow this link for online games:
http://www.epa.gov/epawaste/conserve/materials/textiles.htm#recycle

New from Old

There are many ways to reuse and recycle old textiles. For example:

- Update old items of clothing by using the appliqué technique to sew on scraps of fabric.

- Cut up old or unwanted clothes and other textiles to make materials for a weaving or sculpture.

- Use scraps of fabric to make and stuff soft toys.

- Make jewelry from papier mâché by rolling and twisting strips of paper from magazines to make beads and bangles.

What other ideas can you think of? Could you sell the work you make at a school event and donate your profits to a charity that supports ethical issues?

Glossary

absorbent   able to soak up liquid.

acrylic   a thick, plastic-based paint. Make your own by adding PVA glue to poster paint.

cartoon   in this context, a simple drawing of a sequence of action.

collaboratively   together with other people.

collage   an artwork made by sticking images or fabrics on to a flat surface.

composition   the arrangement of different elements to create a complete artwork.

dye bath   a bucket of ready-to-use dye.

embroider   to decorate by stitching thread on to a textile.

evaluate   to carefully examine and judge something.

felting   the matting together of fibers, usually wool or fur, by heating and squashing them.

fibers   fine threads, for example of cotton.

folk art   art made by people in a particular, often rural, community.

geometric   relating to geometry. Geometry is the area of mathematics that deals with lines, angles, and shapes.

glycerine   a colorless syrup that you can buy at a pharmacy.

horizontally   in a side-to-side position or direction, like the horizon (opposite of vertically).

illustrate   to show with pictures.

insulate   to protect from the cold by using a material to slow the flow of heat.

mask   a material that acts as a screen or block.

mass produce   to make in large quantities, for example in a factory.

metamorphose   to transform into something else.

optical illusion an image that "tricks" the eye.

participate to join in.

pupa (plural **pupae**) the stage when a larva, for example a caterpillar, is changing into an adult, for example a moth.

replica an exact copy.

sketchbook a plain paged book an artist uses to keep visual information to use another time. A sketchbook can be used for note taking, memory jogging, to solve problems or experiment with ideas and techniques.

social group a group of people who come together because of shared interests.

spin to twist short fibers together to make one long strand of yarn.

Stone Age the earliest known period of human culture. Stone Age people made tools out of rocks and stones.

synthetic artificial.

tabard a loose item of clothing that slips over the head and has no sleeves or fastenings.

tapestry a wall hanging in which the threads have been woven into a pattern or picture.

template something that acts as a pattern or mould so that the same image can be reproduced several times.

texture the feel of a surface.

three-dimensional having height, width, and depth.

vertically in an upright position or direction (opposite of horizontally).

visualize to imagine or think of images in your mind.

yarn a continuous strand made from shorter fibers

For Teachers and Parents

This book is ideally placed to help both teachers and imaginative parents as they help children develop a fuller picture of all aspects of textiles.

The ideas and activities are designed to act as starting points for deeper investigation and, in line with the programs of study, it should be remembered that all the activities take place within the process of:

- Exploring and developing ideas.
- Investigating and making art, craft, and design.
- Evaluating and developing work.
- Developing knowledge and understanding.

SUGGESTED FURTHER ACTIVITIES

Pages 4 - 5 What are Textiles?

Teachers can link this investigation linked with work in design and technology, on the one hand, or with any of several science-related topics (for example, heat and warmth, characteristics of materials, or friction).

Make an interactive display of different textiles. Encourage the children to observe the differences in texture and weight. Ask them how these factors contribute to each fabric's use.

Find out all about how textiles are made by going to http://www.childrensuniversity.manchester.ac.uk/interactives/artanddesign/talkingtextiles/

Pages 6 - 7 Spinning and Weaving

The web site http://www.allfiberarts.com is an excellent source of information about textile arts and has a dedicated section on stories that can link to textile projects: http://allfiberarts.com/cs/stories.htm. More myths and legends are at: http://www.snaithprimary.eril.net/ and http://myths.e2bn.org/

Working collaboratively, which is necessary for this weaving activity, has many social benefits for the children, including developing their planning and negotiating skills, as well as confidence in their own abilities.

Pages 8 - 9 Tales from Tapestries

Teachers (or parents) can link these pages with discussions of European history to provide a context for the Bayeux Tapestry.

For single images of the Bayeux Tapestry go to: http://rubens.anu.edu.au/htdocs/bytype/textiles/bayeux/ and to see how a tapestry is created, go to: www.vam.ac.uk/vastatic/microsites/1220_gothic/tapestry_make.php

The children could make flick books showing one event from a scene in the Bayeux Tapestry. Cut several pieces of paper to the same size and staple them together. Draw your images, changing one small action as you progress through each page. Encourage the children to discuss what makes some flick books easier to view than others. Are the images bolder or clearer, or have the small changes to each page been made more carefully?

Pages 10 - 11 Clothes and Fashion

Making imaginative costumes and clothes can be incorporated into a range of topics and set as a challenge over a weekend or school vacation to encourage home-school links. Themes related to topic work, such as "The Environment" or "Inventions," could be alternative starting points. Go to http://vads.ahds.ac.uk/ for images to use on the whiteboard to inspire the children.

The V&A's web site is an excellent source for resources for many of the activities in this book. This link relates directly to clothes and fashion: http://www.vam.ac.uk/collections/fashion/features/index.html

The web site http://www.fashionmuseum.co.uk has interactive quizzes and activities for children as well as information and images useful for teachers and parents.

Pages 12 - 13 What a Performance!

Find out about the Notting Hill Carnival by typing "Carnival" into the search on http://www.mynottinghill.co.uk or view images of carnival and costumes at: http://www.siue.edu/ITDA/CUBA_2004/PHOTOS/carnival.html

Look at the work of Guyanan-born Peter Minshall, who produces some of the world's most exciting carnival costume designs: http://www.callaloo.co.tt

Pages 14 - 15 Investigating Pattern

Patterns found on multicultural artifacts and fabrics, such as saris, are also useful starting points for this topic.

You could help the children to look at patterns in an analytical way to see where the design has derived from, perhaps a natural source. The children could use the Internet or the library to find more examples of patterns from other cultures that are based on nature.

Pages 16 - 17 Patterns for Interior Design

You could link activities that include repeating patterns with math investigations that involve finding patterns and relationships in numbers and shapes. You might explore pattern within rhythms that can be found in music and poetry at the same time as your art project, to make the learning more meaningful.

Collect examples of wallpaper designs from your local hardware store and show the children how a single image is used in a repeating pattern to create a decorative effect.

Using good-quality soft pastels to add detail and highlights on poster-painted surfaces can make the children's work livelier.

Pages 18 - 19 The World of Work

It is important that children make connections between their own learning and the real world of work. Inviting an artist or designer to talk to or work with the children can be stimulating nd inspiring.

Monoprints are a very easy and underrated art activity. Roll some printing ink on to a smooth, flat surface and place some thin newsprint paper on top. Draw your image with a sharp pencil or ballpoint pen, then lift the paper carefully. Don't forget that your image needs to be drawn in reverse. An alternative method is to draw your image into the freshly rolled ink and press paper on to that. This will achieve a negative image. The results of both of these methods always look impressive and beautiful.

Pages 20 - 21 Batik and Tie Dye

The items in this activity will need ironing. If you are allowing children to do this, it is important to make sure they are fully supervised.

Encourage the children to think about the environmental implications of the materials used in dying fabrics. Many traditional materials used for dying are still found in use today, but many of them are under threat because of environmental changes. Look at the web site http://www.pioneerthinking.com/naturaldyes.html to discover the many plants, flowers, and vegetables that can be used to create natural dyes.

Tie dying is an inventive way of adding further interest to lengths of plain material, by tying, folding, twisting or wrapping the fabric before dipping it into dye. The resulting lengths of material can be draped to create quiet areas for reading, or canopies in the outdoor area or playground. Add decoration to tie dyed materials with embroidery or by sewing sequins on to them.

Pages 22 - 23 Quilting and Appliqué

The children could work in pairs to make their appliqué pictures. Show them how to produce different types of stitches, for instance cross-stitch, back-stitch and blanket-stitch, or herringbone. Some good, large images of arpilleras can be seen at: http://www.arpilleras.net/

Pages 24 - 25 The Story of Silk

Find images of Chinese paintings at http://www.chinapage.com/paint1.html and set up an activity where the children can work in a free and loose way to achieve some of the effects.

Encourage children to experiment with watercolor paints and large brushes that will hold a lot of water. Once the watercolor has dried, they can add another layer of paint in some places to achieve some tonal values. When this is dry, the children can add details or lines with thinner brushes and deeper, more intense, colors. Children should be encouraged to enjoy the colous, shapes, patterns, and textures that they produce. This experimental approach will free them from feeling as though they have to produce a "picture."

Pages 26 - 27 Recycling Textiles

Learning about recycling and environmental issues through art and design can be a natural way to open up discussion and set up initiatives in school and at home to raise awareness. http://www.kidsrecycle.org/recycling.php/ has some advice for schools on recycling as well as child-friendly pages to enable independent research.

Visit the online museum of environmental art at: http://greenmuseum.org/

Index